TABLE OF CONTENTS

Introduction – It only takes one time to ruin your life!
Chapter 1 – Be on the Lookout for…
Chapter 2 – Cyberstalking
Chapter 3 – Financial Fraud & Scams
Chapter 4 – Installing Safeguards
Chapter 5 - I Have a Special Gift for My Readers
Meet the Author

Protecting Yourself from Cyber Crime
It only takes one time to ruin your life!
©Copyright 2012 by Dr. Leland Benton

Introduction – It only takes one time to ruin your life!

Cyber criminal activity is increasing at an exponential rate because it is the safest crime to commit. Cyber criminals know that committing cyber crimes below $50,000 are pretty much ignored by law enforcement. Law enforcement is in a big pickle here; it neither has the resources, budget, personnel or expertise to combat cyber crime and apprehend cyber criminals. Like it or not, each individual is left to protect themselves from the lurking cyber criminals and present the hardest target possible so they go off and attack a least prepared individual or business.

Areas of Personal EXPOSURE

- Credit Card Fraud
- Identity Theft
- Financial Scams
- Child Predation
- Computer Hijacking
- Malware
- Spyware
- Viruses
- Keystroke Logging
- Phishing
- User Account & Password Theft
- Cell Phone Spying
- Online Auction Fraud – Ebay, etc.
- And much more…

The above areas of personal exposure are the more prevalent forms of cyber crimes directed against individuals. It is by no means a complete list.

Chapter 1 – Be on the Lookout for...

Surfing the Web

One way that hackers get hold of you is when you surf the web. They put up enticing websites and as soon as you bring one up on your screen they are secretly downloading spyware onto your computer. Here are a few ways to protect yourself when web surfing:

Anonymizer: http://www.anonymizer.com/
Anonymouse: http://www.anonymouse.org/anonwww.html
Identity Cloaker: http://www.identitycloaker.com/?a_aid=neternatives
StartPage: https://www.startpage.com/
Tor Project: https://www.torproject.org/
Freenet Project: https://www.freenetproject.org/

You can also use various proxies to cloak your IP address:

Proxy Heaven: http://www.proxy-heaven.blogspot.com/
Proxy Services: http://www.proxyservices.com/
Your Private Proxy: http://www.yourprivateproxy.com/
HideMyAss: http://www.hidemyass.com/proxy-list/
MyPrivateProxy: http://www.myprivateproxy.net/

Cell Phone Spying

One of the easiest ways to become a victim of cyber-crime is by hacking into your cell phone and installing spyware. Today's Cell Phone spyware does not require that the hacker have possession of your phone. They simply call your cell phone number and whether it is answered or not, it takes all of about 30-seconds to marry your phone to the spyware.

Spyware of this type is readily available on the open market. Go here: http://www.flexispy.com/?ref=1252800

Did you know that with the help of a simple, inexpensive device, anyone with access to your phone could read your private text messages (SMS), even if you have deleted them previously? This device can even recover contacts and a good number or previously dialed numbers. Go here:
http://www.brickhousesecurity.com/cellphone-spy-simcardreader.html

There is also a device that costs a whopping $20 that will tell you the cell phone number of any cell phone within 20-feet of the device. And "NO" we will not tell you where to get one or even what it is called.

The #1 Personal Intrusion is Cell Phone Spying

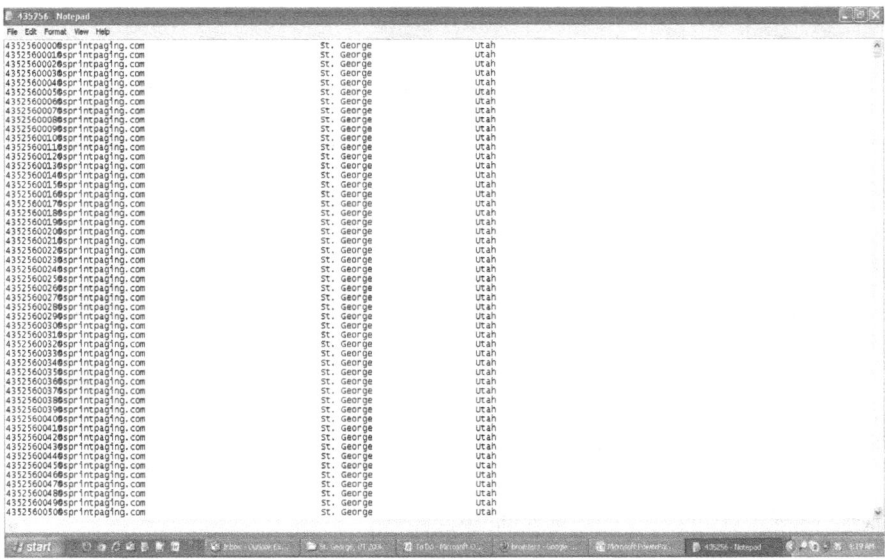

Where do hackers get your cell phone number. See below and the best part is that it is FREE!

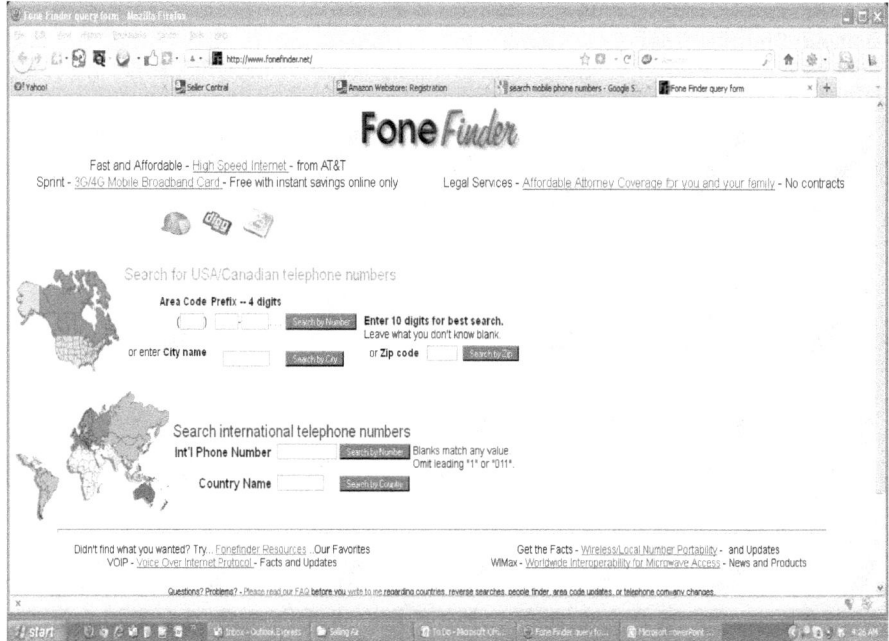

Cell Phone Spying Detection

Your Battery Temperature
One indicator of a possible phone tap is the temperature of your battery. Feel your cell phone if you haven't used it for a while. If it feels warm, this means your phone could be still in use, even if you are not on a call. Please note however that heat may be from overuse. Your battery being hot is only a potential sign if your phone has been powered down for a while.

Phone Not Staying Charged
Having to charge your cell phone more often than normal is another potential sign. If you haven't used it any more than usual, your phone could be in use when you aren't using it. When a cell phone is tapped it loses its battery life faster. A tapped cell phone is constantly recording conversations in the room, even when the phone appears to be idle. You can use an app like BatteryLife LX or Battery LED (iPhone) to monitor your phone's battery life and history over time.

[Note]: Cell phone batteries tend to lose the ability to stay charged over time. If you've had your phone for over a year, your battery may be going bad due to overuse and constant charging over time.

Delay in Shutting Down
When shutting down your phone, if you face issues such as a delay, the back light remaining lit for a time after being shut down, or refusal to shut off, your phone could be tapped. Always be aware of inexplicable activity on your phone. Since phones are made up of hardware and software, however, this could also be caused due to a glitch in the system or some kind of internal problem as well.

More Strange Activity
While turned on, does your phone ever light up, shut down, power up, or install a program on its own? Strange activity could also be a sign of someone else controlling your device.

Note that this can also happen due to interference during the transmission of data.

Background Noise
When on a call, a tapped phone will often include background noises. Usually in the form of echoes, static, or clicking, these sounds can either be caused by interference, a bad connection, or someone else listening in. If you ever hear a pulsating static noise coming from your phone when you are not using it, however, you may have a problem.

Distortion
If you are using your cell phone in close proximity to other electronic devices, like a television, and the other devices become distorted, this could be a sign that additional hardware is installed in the cell phone. A lot of times this distortion is normal, but if it is happening while you're not on a call it could be something to watch for.

What Can You Do About This?
For tips on what you can do if you are ever in this situation, as well as a visual display of some of the signs mentioned above, I invite you to watch this YouTube video entitled, "Is Your Cell Phone Bugged?":

http://www.youtube.com/watch?v=ujosfSkHFrQ

Email

Your email accounts can quite easily be hacked. There is software available on the open market that breaks usernames and passwords. Also, if your computer is hacked, most people leave sensitive information on their computer that can fall into a hackers hands.

To protect your usernames and passwords use Roboform, which is 128-bit encrypted and virtually impossible to hack into:

http://www.roboform.com/php/pums/rfprepay.php?affid=ta556

You can also protect yourself by using a secure email service like Hushmail:

http://www.husmail.com

https://riseup.net/en

http://www.zoho.com/

https://www.hover.com/

Virtual Privacy Networks:

https://www.witopia.net/

https://www.privatvpn.se/en/

http://www.strongvpn.com

Identity Theft

Identity theft occurs when someone uses your personally identifying information, like your name, Social Security number, or credit card number, without your permission, to commit fraud or other crimes. The FTC estimates that as many as 9 million Americans have their identities stolen each year. In fact, you or someone you know may have experienced some form of identity theft.

The crime takes many forms. Identity thieves may rent an apartment, obtain a credit card, or establish a telephone account in your name. You may not find out about the theft until you review your credit report or a credit card statement and notice charges you didn't make—or until you're contacted by a debt collector.

Identity theft is serious. While some identity theft victims can resolve their problems quickly, others spend hundreds of dollars and many days repairing damage to their good name and credit record. Some consumers victimized by identity theft may lose out on job opportunities, or be denied loans for education, housing or cars because of negative information on their credit reports. In rare cases, they may even be arrested for crimes they did not commit.

How do thieves steal an identity?

Identity theft starts with the misuse of your personally identifying information such as your name and Social Security number, credit card numbers, or other financial account information. For identity thieves, this information is as good as gold. Skilled identity thieves may use a variety of methods to get hold of your information, including:

Dumpster Diving. They rummage through trash looking for bills or other paper with your personal information on it.

Skimming. They steal credit/debit card numbers by using a special storage device when processing your card.

Phishing. They pretend to be financial institutions or companies and send spam or pop-up messages to get you to reveal your personal information.

Changing Your Address. They divert your billing statements to another location by completing a change of address form.

Old-Fashioned Stealing. They steal wallets and purses; mail, including bank and credit card statements; pre-approved credit offers; and new checks or tax information. They steal personnel records, or bribe employees who have access.

Pretexting. They use false pretenses to obtain your personal information from financial institutions, telephone companies, and other sources.

What do thieves do with a stolen identity?

Once they have your personal information, identity thieves use it in a variety of ways. Credit card fraud:

They may open new credit card accounts in your name. When they use the cards and don't pay the bills, the delinquent accounts appear on your credit report. They may change the billing address on your credit card so that you no longer receive bills, and then run up charges on your account. Because your bills are now sent to a different address, it may be some time before you realize there's a problem.

Phone or utilities fraud:
They may open a new phone or wireless account in your name, or run up charges on your existing account. They may use your name to get utility services like electricity, heating, or cable TV.

Bank/finance fraud:
They may create counterfeit checks using your name or account number. They may open a bank account in your name and write bad checks. They may clone your ATM or debit card and make electronic withdrawals your name, draining your accounts. They may take out a loan in your name.

Government documents fraud:
They may get a driver's license or official ID card issued in your name but with their picture. They may use your name and Social Security number to get government benefits. They may file a fraudulent tax return using your information.

Other fraud:
They may get a job using your Social Security number. They may rent a house or get medical services using your name. They may give your personal information to police during an arrest. If they don't show up for their court date, a warrant for arrest is issued in your name.

How can you find out if your identity was stolen?

The best way to find out is to monitor your accounts and bank statements each month, and check your credit report on a regular basis. If you check your credit report regularly, you may be able to limit the damage caused by identity theft.

Unfortunately, many consumers learn that their identity has been stolen after some damage has been done. You may find out when bill collection agencies contact you for overdue debts you never incurred. You may find out when you apply for a mortgage or car loan and learn that problems with your credit history are holding up the loan. You may find out when you get something in the mail about an apartment you never rented, a house you never bought, or a job you never held.

What should you do if your identity is stolen?

Filing a police report, checking your credit reports, notifying creditors, and disputing any unauthorized transactions are some of the steps you must take immediately to restore your good name.

Should you file a police report if your identity is stolen?

A police report that provides specific details of the identity theft is considered an Identity Theft Report, which entitles you to certain legal rights when it is provided to the three major credit reporting agencies or to companies where the thief misused your information. An Identity Theft Report can be used to permanently block fraudulent information that results from identity theft, such as accounts or addresses, from appearing on your credit report. It will also make sure these debts do not reappear on your credit reports. Identity Theft Reports can prevent a company from continuing to collect debts that result from identity theft, or selling them to others for collection. An Identity Theft Report is also needed to place an extended fraud alert on your credit report.

You may not need an Identity Theft Report if the thief made charges on an existing account and you have been able to work with the company to resolve the dispute. Where an identity thief has opened new accounts in your name, or where fraudulent charges have been reported to the consumer reporting agencies, you should obtain an Identity Theft Report so that you can take advantage of the protections you are entitled to.

In order for a police report to entitle you to the legal rights mentioned above, it must contain specific details about the identity theft. You should file an ID Theft Complaint with the FTC and bring your printed ID Theft Complaint with you to the police station when you file your police report. The printed ID Theft Complaint can be used to support your local police report to ensure that it includes the detail required.

A police report is also needed to get copies of the thief's application, as well as transaction information from companies that dealt with the thief.

Chapter 2 – Cyberstalking

Cyberstalking is the use of the Internet or other electronic means to stalk or harass an individual, a group of individuals, or an organization. It may include false accusations, monitoring, making threats, identity theft, damage to data or equipment, the solicitation of minors for sex, or gathering information in order to harass. The definition of "harassment" must meet the criterion that a reasonable person, in possession of the same information, would regard it as sufficient to cause another reasonable person distress. Cyberstalking is different from spatial or offline stalking. However, it sometimes leads to it, or is accompanied by it. When identifying cyberstalking and particularly when considering whether to report it to any kind of legal authority, the following features can be considered to characterize a true stalking situation: malice, premeditation, repetition, distress, obsession, vendetta, no legitimate purpose, personally directed, disregarded warnings to stop, harassment, and threats.

A number of key factors have been identified:

False accusations. Many cyberstalkers try to damage the reputation of their victim and turn other people against them. They post false information about them on websites. They may set up their own websites, blogs or user pages for this purpose. They post allegations about the victim to newsgroups, chat rooms or other sites that allow public contributions, such as Wikipedia or Amazon.com.

Attempts to gather information about the victim. Cyberstalkers may approach their victim's friends, family and work colleagues to obtain personal information. They may advertise for information on the Internet, or hire a private detective. They often will monitor the victim's online activities and attempt to trace their IP address in an effort to gather more information about their victims.

Encouraging others to harass the victim. Many cyberstalkers try to involve third parties in the harassment. They may claim the victim has harmed the stalker or his/her family in some way, or may post the victim's name and telephone number in order to encourage others to join the pursuit.

False victimization. The cyberstalker will claim that the victim is harassing him/her. Bocij writes that this phenomenon has been noted in a number of well-known cases.

Attacks on data and equipment. They may try to damage the victim's computer by sending viruses.

Ordering goods and services. They order items or subscribe to magazines in the victim's name. These often involve subscriptions to pornography or ordering sex toys then having them delivered to the victim's workplace.

Arranging to meet. Young people face a particularly high risk of having cyberstalkers try to set up meetings between them.

Types of Cyberstalkers

Of women
Harassment and stalking of women online is common, and can include rape threats and other threats of violence, as well as the posting of women's personal information. It is blamed for limiting victims' activities online or driving them offline entirely, thereby impeding their participation in online life and undermining their autonomy, dignity, identity and opportunities.

Of intimate partners
Cyberstalking of intimate partners is the online harassment of a current or former romantic partner. It is a form of domestic violence, and experts say its purpose is to control the victim in order to encourage social isolation and create dependency. Harassers may send repeated insulting or threatening e-mails to their victims, monitor or disrupt their victims' e-mail use, and use the victim's account to send e-mails to others posing as the victim or to purchase good or services the victim doesn't want. They may also use the internet to research and compile personal information about the victim, to use in order to harass her.

By anonymous online mobs
Web 2.0 technologies have enabled online groups of anonymous people to self-organize to target individuals with online defamation, threats of violence and

technology-based attacks. These include publishing lies and doctored photographs, threats of rape and other violence, posting sensitive personal information about victims, e-mailing damaging statements about victims to their employers, and manipulating search engines to make damaging material about the victim more prominent. Victims are often women and minorities. They frequently respond by adopting pseudonyms or going offline entirely. A notable example of online mob harassment was the experience of American software developer and blogger Kathy Sierra. In 2007, a group of anonymous individuals attacked Sierra, threatening her with rape and strangulation, publishing her home address and Social Security number, and posting doctored photographs of her. Frightened, Sierra cancelled her speaking engagements and shut down her blog, writing "I will never feel the same. I will never be the same."

Experts attribute the destructive nature of anonymous online mobs to group dynamics, saying that groups with homogeneous views tend to become more extreme as members reinforce each other's beliefs, they fail to see themselves as individuals, so they lose a sense of personal responsibility for their destructive acts, they dehumanize their victims, which makes them more willing to behave destructively, and they become more aggressive when they believe they are supported by authority figures. Internet service providers and website owners are sometimes blamed for not speaking out against this type of harassment.

Corporate cyberstalking
Corporate cyberstalking is when a company harasses an individual online, or an individual or group of individuals harasses an organization. Motives for corporate cyberstalking are ideological, or include a desire for financial gain or revenge.

Perpetrators

Profile
Preliminary research has identified four types of cyberstalkers: the vindictive cyberstalkers noted for the ferocity of their attacks; the composed cyberstalker whose motive is to annoy; the intimate cyberstalker who attempts to form a relationship with the victim but turns on them if rebuffed; and collective cyberstalkers, groups with motive. The general profile of the harasser is cold, with little or no respect for others. The stalker is a predator who can wait patiently until vulnerable victims appear, such as women or children, or may enjoy pursuing a particular person, whether personally familiar to them or unknown. The harasser enjoys and demonstrates their power to pursue and psychologically damage the victim.

Behaviors
Cyberstalkers find their victims by using search engines, online forums, bulletin and discussion boards, chat rooms, and more recently, through social networking sites, such as MySpace, Facebook, Bebo, Friendster, Twitter, and Indymedia, a media outlet known for self-publishing.

They may engage in live chat harassment or flaming or they may send electronic viruses and unsolicited e-mails. Cyberstalkers may research individuals to feed their obsessions and curiosity. Conversely, the acts of cyberstalkers may become more intense, such as repeatedly instant messaging their targets. More commonly they will post defamatory or derogatory statements about their stalking target on web pages, message boards and in guest books designed to get a reaction or response from their victim, thereby initiating contact. In some cases, they have been known to create fake blogs in the name of the victim containing defamatory or pornographic content.

When prosecuted, many stalkers have unsuccessfully attempted to justify their behavior based on their use of public forums, as opposed to direct contact. Once they get a reaction from the victim, they will typically attempt to track or follow the victim's internet activity. Classic cyberstalking behavior includes the tracing of the victim's IP address in an attempt to verify their home or place of employment.

Some cyberstalking situations do evolve into physical stalking, and a victim may experience abusive and excessive phone calls, vandalism, threatening or obscene mail, trespassing, and physical assault. Moreover, many physical stalkers will use cyberstalking as another method of harassing their victims.

Chapter 3 – Financial Fraud & Scams

Are There Anyways of Overcoming Cyber Fraud?

Internet is the fastest growing medium on earth that you would find these days and for everything it is the best solution that people consider looking into. Where it has all the benefits and advantages like communication, link building, advertisement, online movie downloads, online song downloads, emailing, instant messaging and searching out the concerns and issues there are plenty of things that internet has got wrong as well. There are multiple different kinds of internet scams and frauds that are out there that you have to be careful from. It is something that has been bothering individuals ever since internet was introduced and many times, simple things could make you a victim when you won't even get to know of it.

The email scam is at the top of the internet scams and internet fake activities. People have had a routine of making money from different resources. You might have been through those false emails and messages that come into your inbox saying you won a lottery or you just made thousands of dollars from some resource which you don't even know of. These cyber fraud emails are often auto generated and are sent out to hundreds of people like you so they could enter their account information and even simple money transactions for those people to take benefits from. After paying the processing fee to the scammed email, the individuals would get no suitable response to it and they would rather be asked for the bank account information and different sort of things that could lead the scam artists to the big amount of money and funds.

You can stop cyber fraud by reporting them to the local police and even to the online websites that have an option to do so. Most of the time, people don't consider reporting such things because they are considered unimportant; this is the main reason why scammers are getting more confidence towards what they are doing. One of the other causes due to which this cyber fraud is spreading day by day is because people overlook the cyber laws and regulations that are made out by the websites and forums. People should get to know more about internet laws and what to do once they find out someone is not abiding by them in an effective manner. One should take out significant amount of time checking the emails and several other notifications online to see which ones are valid and which ones aren't.

Cyber fraud refers to any type of deliberate deception for unfair or unlawful gain that occurs online. The most common form is online credit card theft. Other common forms of monetary cyber fraud include nondelivery of paid products purchased through online auctions and nondelivery of merchandise or software bought online. Cyber fraud also refers to data break-ins, identity theft, and cyberbullying, all of which are seriously damaging.

Here's an example: A 20-year-old Facebook user posted: *"I eyed this girl on campus for months before I finally got the nerve to talk to her. I created an excuse to ask her a question and then started chatting her up. I must have given off the vibe that I was interested because right away, she dropped the bomb that she had a boyfriend. Bummed but not discouraged, I got my computer-savvy friend to hack into her boyfriend's Facebook account and change his relationship status to 'single.' The girl must have freaked out because the next thing I heard, they'd gotten into a huge fight and broken things off. A few days later, I asked her about her boyfriend, totally playing it off like I had no idea they were through. When she told me what had happened, I offered to take her out for coffee to get her mind off the breakup. My plan worked, because after our little date, she came back to my dorm room and we hooked up."*

Not all cyber fraud occurs through e-mail, but most of them do. Other methods are on the Internet itself. You may even get a letter through the post, because your postal address may have been captured by a spyware program or spam e-mail you replied to with your postal address included in the reply. Most scams exploit people's greediness. There is always promise of great returns on money you should invest in them. You can stay safe by following common sense and a few basic simple rules:

- Never send people money that contacted you by e-mail, or any other method in the Internet, period. Especially if you never heard of them before. What clear minded person will send money to a complete stranger?
- Never reply to, or click on any links in e-mails requesting personal, account or any kind of user information.
- Never reply to, or click on any links in e-mails from organizations you are not member of. Why will Amazon, PayPal, eBay, Barclays Bank, or any organization send you e-mail if you are not a member of them?
- Never reply to, or click on any links in lottery or competition e-mails, you never entered. How can you suddenly win a competition you never entered?

Another way to identify fraud is looking at the real URL the link in the e-mail points to. How do I do that? Well most of the popular e-mail clients have a status bar at the bottom of your screen. If you hover with your mouse cursor above the link, the URL (Uniform Resource Locator, in other words, the exact web address it points to) will appear in the status bar. These links should point to the main domain of the company.

For instance the links in e-mail from PayPal should start with www.paypal.com, nothing else. If it starts with something like www.pay-pal.com, www.pay.pal.com, www.paypal_.com, www.paypalsecure.com or any variation of the real domain, then it's fraudulent, even if it points to a secure server (These links start with https:// and not the standard http://).

Any variation of the real domain points to a different server, not owned by PayPal, where you can get infected by viruses, spyware, adware, or become victim of a hacking attempt.

What is the #1 Internet Scam today?

U.S. Colleges and Universities Most Favored Target for Phishing

Phishing attacks against colleges and universities are focused on stealing the login credentials that students use to access all their personal university-related information and email; credentials that usually consist of students' usernames and passwords. Why phishers are seeking out students' information?

1. Young naïve girls ripe for cyberstalking and;
2. Application for financial aid or bogus student loans, as demonstrated by a recent case in Arizona.

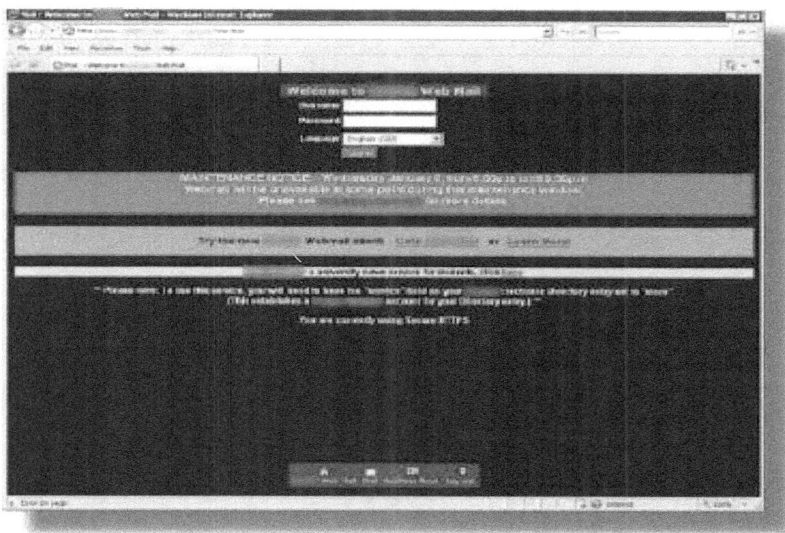

Phishing attack masquerading as a University's Webmail portal

Phishing attack disguised as a University's login page

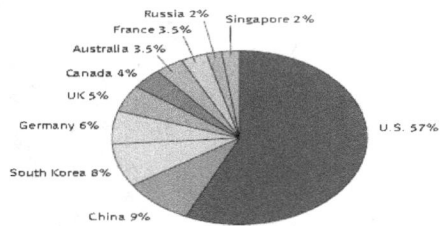

Top Ten Countries Hosting Phishing Attacks

Computer Hijacking

Computer Hijacking is a crime where the criminal takes over your computer and you are unable to control anything that is being done to your computer. This is a federal offence and the criminal will be jailed if caught.

How to protect against computer hijacking and against theft of your personal data (with potential to be used in Identity Theft).

Hijacking can only happen when hijacker's software finds its way to your computer. Identity theft comes with unauthorized access to your information.

So the best way to protect is :

Don't let them in!

Keep out software that you do not trust, *such as*:
- Any suspicious e-mail attachments
- Files downloaded from strange places
- ActiveX and Plugins from untrusted sites
- Use Spyware

To achieve **this you need**
- Several building blocks to be in place:
- Patch your browsers.
- Antivirus product.
- Anti spyware product.
- Personal firewall

You should look after your protection software:

- Keep them up-to-date.
- Check them regularly (for example - weekly) that automatic update is really working.
- Configure your software (like antivirus) to scan your computer daily (at night or at lunch time)

Keep software on your computers patched. Attackers would not be able to exploit known vulnerabilities and execute their programs through security holes.

To achieve that –

- Keep and maintain list of software you have installed
- Check for updates for each package regularly. Switch ON automatic checking for updates whenever it is possible.
- Note: Do you use MS Office? When did you check for MS Office update last time? Burn critical updates, Service Packs, Product Releases etc. on the two blank CDs

and store one on site and one off site. *List of what I think is critical for the current versions of Windows OS could be found on this site soon.*

Keep you data safe and available for restore in case that something does happen.

You will need your important information be available ASAP.

To achieve this -

- Identify data that should be preserved
- Keep your business related data files (such as drawings, plans, documents, presentations, program, schedules, lists of customers) in well identified places on your hard drive (or server)
- Check where is your e-mail program keeps your mail box and address book.
- Back up that data regularly.
- Check that backed up data can be restored correctly and actually used. Do it regularly
- Store back up media outside your main office.

This would help as part of any disaster. Power failure could destroy your hard drives. Thieves could steal your computers. You would need your data to keep business running.

So to make a conclusion:

Create the list what should be done and how often. Check that it is achievable
Make schedule out of it. Put it in your dairy (electronic or paper). Follow it
Review it when necessary.

Keystroke Logging - Phishing

Keystroke logging (often called **keylogging**) is the action of tracking (or logging) the keys struck on a keyboard, typically in a covert manner so that the person using the keyboard is unaware that their actions are being monitored. There are numerous keylogging methods, ranging from hardware and software-based approaches to electromagnetic and acoustic analysis.

Software-based keyloggers
A logfile from a software-based keylogger
A control window from a software-based keylogger
These are software programs designed to work on the target computer's operating system. From a technical perspective there are five categories:

Hypervisor-based: The keylogger can theoretically reside in a malware hypervisor running underneath the operating system, which remains untouched. It effectively becomes a virtual machine. Blue Pill is a conceptual example.

Kernel-based: This method is difficult both to write and to combat. Such keyloggers reside at the kernel level and are thus difficult to detect, especially for user-mode applications. They are frequently implemented as rootkits that subvert the operating system kernel and gain unauthorized access to the hardware, making them very powerful. A keylogger using this method can act as a keyboard device driver for example, and thus gain access to any information typed on the keyboard as it goes to the operating system.

API-based: These keyloggers hook keyboard APIs; the operating system then notifies the keylogger each time a key is pressed and the keylogger simply records it. Windows APIs such as GetAsyncKeyState, GetForegroundWindow, etc. are used to poll the state of the keyboard or to subscribe to keyboard events. These types of keyloggers are the easiest to write, but where constant polling of each key is required, they can cause a noticeable increase in CPU usage, and can also miss the occasional key. A more recent example simply polls the BIOS for pre-boot authentication PINs that have not been cleared from memory.

Form grabbing based: Form grabbing-based keyloggers log web form submissions by recording the web browsing onsubmit event functions. This records form data before it is passed over the Internet and bypasses HTTPS encryption.

Memory injection based: Memory Injection (MITB)-based keyoggers alter memory tables associated with the browser and other system functions to perform their logging functions. By patching the memory tables or injecting directly into memory, this technique can be used by malware authors who are looking to bypass Windows UAC (User Account Control). The Zeus and Spyeye Trojans use this method exclusively.

Packet analyzers: This involves capturing network traffic associated with HTTP POST events to retrieve unencrypted passwords.

Remote access software keyloggers - These are local software keyloggers with an added feature that allows access to the locally recorded data from a remote location. Remote communication may be achieved using one of these methods:

- Data is uploaded to a website, database or an FTP server.
- Data is periodically emailed to a pre-defined email address.
- Data is wirelessly transmitted by means of an attached hardware system.

The software enables a remote login to the local machine from the Internet or the local network, for data logs stored on the target machine to be accessed.

Used by police - In 2000, the FBI used a keystroke logger to obtain the PGP passphrase of Nicodemo Scarfo, Jr., son of mob boss Nicodemo Scarfo. Also in 2000, the FBI lured two suspected Russian cyber criminals to the US in an elaborate ruse, and captured their usernames and passwords with a keylogger that was covertly installed on a machine that they used to access their computers in Russia. The FBI then used these credentials to hack into the suspects' computers in Russia in order to obtain evidence to prosecute them.

Countermeasures - The effectiveness of countermeasures varies, because keyloggers use a variety of techniques to capture data and the countermeasure needs to be effective against the particular data capture technique. For example, an on-screen keyboard will be effective against hardware keyloggers, transparency will defeat some screenloggers - but not all - and an anti-spyware application that can only disable hook-based keyloggers will be ineffective against kernel-based keyloggers.

Also, keylogger software authors may be able to update the code to adapt to countermeasures that may have proven to be effective against them.

Anti keyloggers - An anti keylogger is a piece of software specifically designed to detect keyloggers on your computer, typically comparing all files in your computer against a database of keyloggers looking for similarities which might signal the presence of a hidden keylogger. As anti keyloggers have been designed specifically to detect keyloggers, they have the potential to be more effective than conventional anti virus software; some anti virus software do not consider certain keyloggers a virus, as under some circumstances a keylogger can be considered a legitimate piece of software.

User Account – Password Theft

Use a password management program, which stores all of my passwords safely under one master password.

The key is to make sure you have a strong master password for your password management program to protect your list of passwords. You'll want to create strong passwords for each site that you log into as well.

A strong password must have at least 8 characters (the longer the better), with a mixture of upper and lower-case letters, numbers and, if the site or service allows, special characters, such as "!," "#" and "?." It should be something you can remember easily. A long sentence works well when you take the first letter of each word and then substitute the vowels for numbers or symbols.

For example: The quick brown fox jumped inside the orange box and slept = Tqbfj1t0b&s

Once you've created your master password, you can set up your password manager. It stores your passwords and user names in an encrypted database, enabling you to quickly access them. Once you have your password manager running, it fills in your user ID and password for you.

The free Mozilla Firefox Web browser for PCs and Macs has a built-in password manager, but you need to make sure you create a master password to protect your list. Other browsers — Internet Explorer, Safari and Chrome — can remember passwords for you, but they do not have a manager or master password to protect your passwords, so it's best to use a dedicated program.

For stand-alone password managers, one of the best is RoboForm Everywhere, which works with Macs and PCs, as well as iPhones and Android phones. The program can auto-fill just about any online form, including email, name, phone number and credit card information.

http://www.roboform.com/php/pums/rfprepay.php?affid=ta556

And for Macs (and PCs), check out 1Password ($49.95 at agilewebsolutions.com). The software saves passwords, credit card numbers, account registration information, just about anything you can think of, and auto-fills it all across most browsers on a Mac, including Safari, Firefox and Camino.

There's also an app for iPhone and iPad ($9.99 in iTunes) that will sync with your desktop and stop you from having to peck out your passwords on that tiny touchscreen keyboard.

Hard Drive & Disc Encryption
Hacking your hard drive and other data storage devices can be preventing by using a free disc encryption program called TrueCrypt:

http://www.truecrypt.org/docs/

TRUECRYPT
FREE OPEN-SOURCE ON-THE-FLY ENCRYPTION

TrueCrypt encrypts everything on your hard drive and all your personal information and is virtually impossible to bust into and hack.

Here are a few more encryption providers:

http://www.endoacustica.com/index_en.htm
http://www.hotspotshield.com/

Miscellaneous Protection

The Best Firewall: http://www.comodo.com/

Stop Unwanted Mail: https://www.catalogchoice.org/

Secure Mailing Address: http://www.earthclassmail.com/

Secure VOIP Phone: http://zfoneproject.com/

Secure Chat Room: https://crypto.cat/

You can review chat room logs using this: http://www.pimall.com/nais/chatstick.html#

You can detect PORN on any computer instantly:

http://www.pimall.com/nais/porndetectionstick.html#

Identify weaknesses and vulnerabilities in your personal computer:

http://www.eeye.com/products/retina/retina-network-scanner

Secure Search Engine

http://duckduckgo.com/

Privacy Apps for your browser

http://news.ghostery.com/
http://abine.com/dntdetail.php

Chapter 4 – Installing Safeguards

Lost? Attacked? Abducted? Injured? Disaster?

Pinpoint Protection from PinpointProtect Offers Two Exclusive Programs!

Pinpoint Protect Guardian

There are always situations that a person finds him/herself in that they cannot control. PinpointProtect is here to assist you when you need help. If you become lost, attacked, abducted, injured or have suffered through a disaster, we know where you are and we can send help.

We know where you are because our proprietary GPS technology locates your exact position within 10-yards and can send help.

We know if you are in trouble because all you have to do is push the "SOS" button and we go into action.

24/7 Monitoring

We monitor our customers 24/7 through a state-of-the-art central control room where we scan the globe watching…ready to spring into action whenever we are needed.

It doesn't matter where you are in the world; it doesn't matter how remote a location; the weather doesn't affect our ability to find you; even if all services are down and unavailable, Pinpoint Protection is still working and still able to pinpoint your exact location.

Password-Protected Internet Interface

You may not know where you are but we do! And everybody you give a username/password can pinpoint your exact location using our Password-Protected Internet Interface.

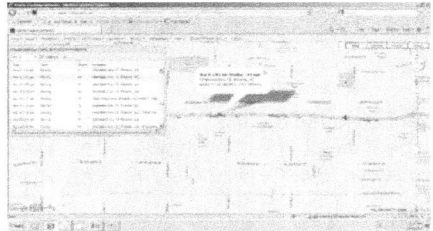

If you are lost, you too can go on the Internet and find your location…and anyone else that you give permission to locate you. Again, it doesn't matter where you are in the world or the weather conditions; we always know where you are and so does anybody else that you give permission to know.

Likely Scenarios where Pinpoint Protect Guardian can help:

High Profile People – people with high profiles: movie stars, sports figures, wealthy people, government figures, etc need extra protection and PinpointProtect gives them that special peace-of-mind.

Lost – everybody becomes lost eventually. It doesn't even have to be somewhere that is remote; if you are lost you can hit the SOS button or if you have access to the Internet, you can find your exact location.

Attacked – women are especially vulnerable to attack and eventually find themselves in situations where an attack is made easier such as parking garages, elevators, dark streets, parking lots. Just hit the SOS button and we send the cavalry.

Abducted – unfortunately, abduction and kidnapping has become a cottage industry in many parts of the world, especially in Mexico, Central and South America. If you live or travel to any parts of the world where this is common you need PinpointProtect!

Injured – In any situation where you are injured, even if you cannot push the SOS button, we at least know where you are and can send help.

Disaster – you can be buried under rubble and we still can locate you. You may not be able to communicate with the outside world because all communication facilities are down but your family can know where you are and if you are moving by logging into the Internet Interface.

Travel – no matter where you go or where you travel to, PinpointProtect goes with you and gives your loved ones peace-of-mind knowing exactly where you are at all times. They can even know if you arrived at your destination by using the Internet Interface.

Work – do you have a job where you work alone or in a remote location? With PinpointProtect, you are NEVER alone! We are there with you at all times.

Dating – date rape and violence against women is becoming all too common. How does a woman protect herself? Yep…PinpointProtect! Now if a lady needs help she can push the SOS button and we send help to her exact location. But this doesn't mean that a lady should not be prudent and do all she can to protect herself.

Banking – If you take daily deposits to the bank for your business, you need PinpointProtect! Don't be foolish enough to think that no one is watching you and logging the times and routes you take to the bank. Plan for the worst but hope for the best!

Elderly – oddly enough, most of the "lost" calls we

receive are for elderly people. With the advent of electric wheelchairs (scooters) the elderly have a tendency to wander. They are easily disoriented and need help. With PinpointProtect, it is easy to find them and bring them home. Also the SOS button is there in case they need help for whatever reason.

Teens – the best description for teens are "walking hormones with feet"! Let's face it; the world presents way too many opportunities for teens to get into trouble. One would think that teens resent PinpointProtect. Not so; our surveys show that they actually appreciate having the ability to communicate when they are in trouble and know that their parents know where they are at all times.

College – PinpointProtect gives parents that extra peace-of-mind when their kids go off to college. Knowing where they are and where they are supposed to be and also knowing that when they get into trouble or a scary situation that they have a way to communicate is comforting to parents whose kid(s) are out of the nest for the first time.

Hunting – all hunting takes place in remote locations and many times in locations where cell phones do not work. Never go hunting without PinpointProtect!

Driving/Commuting – no matter where you drive or how long a commute PinpointProtect goes along with you. Even if cell phone service isn't available,

PinpointProtect is always available.

Here is how we do it...

The Problem: the biggest problem concerning GPS tracking devices is the battery life. Most GPS tracking devices are only used for specific surveillance for a short period of time and hence; the battery life is only a few hours.

The Solution: Our proprietary tracking unit works on motion and will conserve battery power when a person is not moving. The unit has a battery life of 30 hours depending on the reporting rate you choose.

This is important! First, our unit goes to sleep as long as you are stationary. The minute you start moving, it wakes up and reports your coordinates. This feature saves the battery life and allows our unit up to 3-days usage until it needs to be recharged (the unit comes with a charger and it works just like your cell phone charger).

Second, our PinpointProtect proprietary software in our control room automatically notifies our personnel when you have been stationary for an unusually long period of time. Our personnel check your location first to determine if there is a good reason that you have been stationary. For example, if you are in New York and you have been stationary after 8 PM then we assume you are sleeping.

However; if you are in the remote desert of New Mexico and have been stationary for over 8-hours our personnel will attempt to make contact with you. If we cannot make contact then we will call the contact people on your application and inquire if they have been in communication with you.

Furthermore – there is no reason for the unit to be turned off. Even when it is charging the unit can remain on. Our PinpointProtect proprietary software in our control room automatically notifies our personnel when any unit is turned off and we immediately attempt to make contact. Again, if we cannot make contact then we will call the contact people on your application and inquire if they have been in communication with you.

Note – a customer can turned the unit off at any time if they do not want their location known. This is your choice. If so, we provide a phone number to our control room to notify our personnel that you are turning off the unit so we do not react.

Peace of mind – Knowing that PinpointProtect personnel are just a phone call away is very comforting. For whatever reason, you can always call us for assistance and our personnel will respond.

You are never alone with PinpointProtect!

The hardware that makes it all work…

The Spark Nano 3.0 for Adults

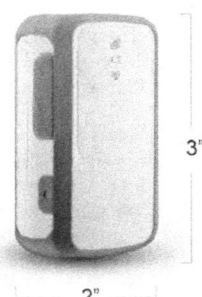

$199.95 + $14.95/month monitoring

PinpointProtect offers the latest tracking unit that is specifically designed with personal tracking and safety in mind. The Spark Nano 3.0 is the most intuitive, cost-effective, and customizable real-time tracker on the market today. Small enough to fit in the palm of your hand, the Nano is perfect for tracking people, vehicles, or assets. View your target's location 24/7 and get live alerts directly from your computer or smartphone.

For Children – Lok8u

$199 + $9.99/month monitoring

Designed specifically to be worn by kids; it is waterproof and resembles a popular children's digital watch (24 hr clock display). It is also tamper-proof and virtually impossible to remove because it requires special release tool (included). It has a built-in tamper-sensor that sends an alert to your cell phone or PC if GPS locator is removed. You can even send a text message "Where R U" to the GPS locator to receive location updates right on your smartphone. The unit keeps tracking your child when GPS signal is lost via cell-tower triangulation. The unit has personalize GPS tracking settings; "Standby" or "Live Track" alerts and it is now available in two colors; pink or black.

For Pets – Tagg the Pet Tracker

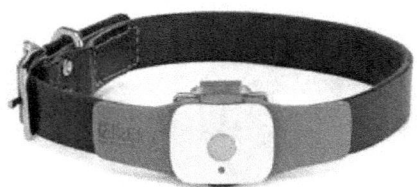

$199.95 includes 1-year of service
The goal of the Tagg system isn't just to find a lost dog - it's to not lose him in the first place. The lightweight dog GPS device attaches to most collars and lets you locate and track your dog using a computer or smartphone. The simple set-up procedure allows you to create your very own Tagg zone, the area where your dog spends most of his time. If he isn't where he's supposed to be, you'll know.

PinpointProtect is an expensive operation to offer and maintain...

Providing the PinpointProtect service is costly. We are able to offer our services at affordable prices because PinpointProtect has three sister divisions that use our services too and we spread the costs out to bring the economies-to-scale in line.

SurvivalNations.com – is our disaster/crisis preparation division where we form what we call PrepperNation groups and teach survival preparation and planning. Each group leader accounts for each PrepperNation member in the event of a disaster and crisis using PinpointProtect's services.

ForensicsNation.com – is our investigative/security unit involved in Internet/Computer forensics and online security. They use PinpointProtect's services to find and locate cyber criminals worldwide. You can run but you cannot hide because ForensicsNation is always watching.

PrivacyNations.com – offer a person the ability to remain private and provides resources and education in how to protect privacy. Privacy is a very important issue with PinpointProtect. Our service is not meant to invade a person's privacy and we are all too aware that it can be abused. We have built-in safeguards to protect your privacy too. Our Password-Protected Internet Interface is designed where you can grant or revoke permission at any time to anybody you allow access to it. On your application for service you list your contact people and whether or not PinpointProtect is allowed to share information with them. If no one is listed then PinpointProtect will only share your information with emergency services in time of need.

To Order PinpointProtect:

The cost of PinpointProtect is $9.95 per month. The customer purchases the applicable hardware unit(s) directly from the manufacturer at the prices listed below and PinpointProtect's fee is for 24/7 monitoring:

The Spark Nano 3.0 Unit - $199.95 + a monitoring fee of $14.95/month

The Lok8u Child's Unit - $199 + a monitoring fee$9.95/month

The Tagg Pet Unit - $199.95 and this includes 1-year of monitoring

PinpointProtect requires a minimum 12-month contract. We require an ACH automatic withdrawal of the monthly fee from your credit/debit card or your bank account so that PinpointProtect's service is never interrupted.

ForensicsNation/PinpointProtect
support@neternatives.com
435-249-5600

Chapter 5 - I Have a Special Gift for My Readers

I appreciate my readers for without them I am just another struggling author attempting to make ends meet.

My readers and I have in common a passion for the written word as well as the desire to learn and grow from books. My special offer to you is a massive ebook library that I have compiled over the years. It contains hundreds of fiction and non-fiction ebooks in Adobe Acrobat PDF format as well as the Greek classics and old literary classics too.

In fact, this library is so massive to completely download the entire library will require over 5 GBs open on your desktop. Use the link below and scan all of the ebooks in the library. You can select the ebooks you want individually or download the entire library.

The link below does not expire after a given time period so you are free to return for more books rather than clog your desktop. And feel free to give the link to your friends who enjoy reading too.

I thank you for reading my book and hope if you are pleased that you will leave me an honest review so that I can improve my work and or write books that appeal to your interests.

Okay, here is the link...

http://tinyurl.com/special-readers-promo

PS: If you wish to reach me personally for any reason you may simply write to mailto:support@epubwealth.com.

I answer all of my emails so rest assured I will respond.

NOTE: All of the downloadable files in the massive ebook library have been scanned by eSet.com NOD 32 Antivirus 5 and are virus free!

Meet the Author

Dr. Leland Benton is Director of Applied Web Info, a leading Internet Marketing company based in Utah. With over 21,000 resellers in over 22-countries, its operating entity - Neternatives.com - is a leader in Information Technology and online marketing. He is also a behavioral scientist and Chief Forensics Investigator for ForensicsNation.com. Leland resides in Southern Utah.

Visit some of his websites
http://appliedmindsciences.com/
http://appliedwebinfo.com/
http://bookbuilderplus.com
http://embarrassingproblemsfix.com/
http://www.epubwealth.com/
http://forensicsnation.com/
http://www.freebiesnation.com/
http://neternatives.com/
http://privacynations.com/
http://refernationwordofmouth.com/
http://survivalnations.com/
http://texternation.com/
http://thebentonkitchen.com
http://theolegions.org
http://willilookgoodinthis.com

www.ingramcontent.com/pod-product-compliance
Lightning Source LLC
Chambersburg PA
CBHW070724180526
45167CB00004B/1601